HEALTHY
&DELICIOUS

**More than 50 nutritious and super tasty recipes
to inspire you to live a healthy lifestyle**

Priscilla Sousa & Raquel Britzke

Introduction

The brilliant idea of this book came from the need to develop a whole new and fantastic slimming programme, the 'PFD Reset.' Raquel wanted something new and exciting for her patients. She became an admirer of Priscilla's creations and decided to invite her to write this special book.

The purpose of this cookbook is to transform your life in the kitchen and to change your views about dieting. It has a unique combination of your everyday ingredients and the nutrition facts you need to ensure you are following a well-balanced diet.

Priscilla will share the step-by-step of her wonderful creations which will not only inspire your cooking but will also motivate your family to follow you in your healthy eating journey. Raquel will make sure you have the correct portion and nutrients needed for a perfectly balanced diet.

Priscilla and Raquel will show you that you can eat most ingredients and obtain fantastic creations and results while following a diet.

This book will bring simplicity to what sometimes seems so complicated. It will prove that everyone can create something incredibly delicious from simple ingredients!

This book is dedicated to all the incredible women who are forever trying to be the best version of themselves.

Priscilla Sousa

Raquel Britzke

Priscilla has lived in the UK for 20 years, adopting London as her homeland. She has a degree in Finance and is a Manager in Business Analysis and Software Designer in a multinational...Yes you read it correctly... let's move to chapter 2 please...

Her passion for gastronomy started when she was a General Manager of prestigious fine dining restaurants in London for 14 years; she learnt from the best chefs.

With the invitation to write this book, Priscilla will share her passion, knowledge and inspiring ideas. She would like to ensure people understand how easy it is to cook incredible dishes and still be able to follow a diet.

Raquel Britzke is a nutritionist with over 13 years of experience, certified as a personal trainer and postgraduate in sports nutrition by the International Olympic Committee.

She founded Britzke Nutrition Clinic in London, England, where she lives with her family. She has also created several successful weight loss programs using her own method and helping more than 15,000 patients around the world.

Her passion and mission has been to transform people's lives through dietary re-education, enabling weight loss, muscle mass gain and a much healthier and happier lifestyle.

Table Of Content

Table Of Content

Breakfast

Low Carb Almond Bread

Time: 30 minutes
10 Portions

Ingredients

- 3 Eggs
- 150g Ground Almonds or Almond Flour
- 3 tbsp Greek Yoghurt or Natural Yoghurt
- 1 tbsp Parmesan Cheese
- 1 tbsp Baking Powder
- Salt
- Oregano - don't be shy, it's delicious!
- Chia Seeds
- Sunflower Seeds
- Linseed and Pumpkin Seeds to put on top

Method

Step 1
Before you start your preparation, preheat the oven to 180°C. Mix all ingredients with a spoon. Add the baking powder last.

Step 2
Grease a rectangular baking tray. Add the bread mixture to the tray. Add the pumpkin seeds and linseeds on the top.

Bake it for 15-20 minutes.

Nutrition Facts	Per Portion (40 g)
Energy	147 kcal
Protein	7g
Carbohydrate	1g
Sugars	0g
Fat	12g
Fatty Acids, Total Saturated	1g
Fibres	2g
Sodium	281mg

Cloud Bread

Cloud Bread

Ingredients

- 3 Eggs
- 2 tbsp Cottage Cheese or Cream Cheese
- 1/2 tbs Bicarbonate Soda
- Salt
- Few drops of Lemon Juice or Vinegar

Method

Step 1
Preheat your oven to 170°C. Get a large glass or stainless-steel bowl – the material of the bowl you'll be whipping your whites in is extremely important. NEVER ever beat egg whites in a plastic bowl. Plastic retains oils like a sponge and will leave you with weepy, broken up whites.

As a safe-guard, lightly dab a paper towel with vinegar and wipe your whisk and bowl interior to reduce the possibility of your egg whites breaking.

Now, separate your whites while being extremely careful not to let any yolks in.

Step 2
Once you have your egg whites, place them into the bowl and start whisking them with an electric whisk.

Add the pinch of salt here. Start beating at a low speed (speed 2) until the whites start becoming frothy.

Egg whites are very delicate, so always start beating them at a slow speed. Then gradually increase it as they begin to froth and increase in size.

This is the very first stage of beating whites. After about a minute or so, the whites should be filled with tiny bubbles that have developed since we started incorporating air into them with the whisk.

Step 3
After reaching this frothy stage, add in cream a few drops of lemon juice. Most recipes typically call for a couple of drops of lemon juice/vinegar. Increase the mixer speed to medium (speed 4 to 6) and continue beating.

Step 4

Now on a separate recipient, add the yolks with the cheese until it becomes very creamy and smooth. Then, incorporate the mixture into the egg whites delicately with a wooden spoon or a spatula.

Nutrition Facts	Per Portion (90 g)
Energy	115 kcal
Protein	10g
Carbohydrate	1g
Sugars	1g
Fat	7g
Fatty Acids, Total Saturated	3g
Fibres	0g
Sodium	947mg

Cheesy Bread

Time: 10 minutes
2 Portions

Ingredients

- 4 tbsp Tapioca Starch
- 1 Egg
- 1 tbsp of Cottage Cheese or Ricotta
- 20g Parmesan Cheese
- 1 tsp Salt

Method

Step 1
Mix all the ingredients until it gets homogeneous and creamy.

Step 2
Place a non-stick frying pan on high heat. Add some coconut oil and put the mixture into the pan. Let it get firm and golden, then turn to make the other side golden.

Tip: If you cannot find Tapioca Starch, please use 2 tablespoons of Tapioca Flour (instead of 4) and 1 additional egg.

Nutrition Facts	Per Portion (98 g)
Energy	242 kcal
Protein	9g
Carbohydrate	37g
Sugars	1g
Fat	7g
Fatty Acids, Total Saturated	3g
Fibres	0g
Sodium	1166mg

Low Carb Bread, Avocado and Poached Eggs

Low-Carb Bread, Avocado, and Poached Eggs

Ingredients

- 1 slice of Low-Carb Almond Bread - see the recipe in the book
- 1/2 Avocado
- 1 tsp Olive Oil
- 2 Eggs, small
- 1 tsp Vinegar
- Chilli Flakes

Method

Step 1
Smash the avocado with a fork, add olive oil, salt and black pepper.

Step 2
Now it is time to poach your egg – see step by step below:

Poached Egg

1. First, put water in a small, deep pot to boil. When it is boiling, completely lower the heat to the minimum to have small bubbles on the bottom. Place a tablespoon of vinegar in the water.

2. Place the raw egg in a fine-mesh strainer over a bowl. The very thin egg whites will run through the sieve. What was left in the sieve you can put in a glass or cup, and the thin egg whites can be discarded.

3. Stir the water with a spoon and add the egg gently to the hot water.

4. Turn off the heat and cover the pan (or lower the heat to low) and cook for 4 minutes until the egg whites are cooked. (You may need to add more time if you cook at altitude or poach more than 4 eggs at a time.)

Step 3
Once the poached eggs are ready, it is time to assemble.

Take a slice of bread, put the avocado on top, then place the eggs on top of the avocado. Sprinkle a little salt, black pepper, and some chilli flakes.

Nutrition Facts	Per Portion (283 g)
Energy	474 kcal
Protein	17g
Carbohydrate	33g
Sugars	2g
Fat	33g
Fatty Acids, Total Saturated	6g
Fibres	14g
Sodium	440mg

Shakshuka

Ingredients

- 1 Onion, small and diced
- Red Bell Pepper, seeded and diced
- 2 Garlic Cloves, finely chopped
- 1 tsp Paprika
- 1/2 tsp Cumin
- 1/4 tsp Chilli Powder
- 350g Tomatoes, peeled
- 4 Eggs, large
- Salt and Pepper to taste
- 1 small bunch of fresh Coriander, chopped
- 1 small bunch of fresh Parsley, chopped
- 30g Feta Cheese
- 1 Avocado, small tbsp of Olive Oil

Method

Step 1
Heat olive oil in a large sauté pan on medium heat. Add the chopped bell pepper and onion and cook for 5 minutes or until the onion becomes translucent.

Add garlic and spices and cook for an additional minute. Pour the peeled tomatoes and juice into the pan and break down the tomatoes using a large spoon. Season with salt and pepper and bring the sauce to a simmer.

Step 2
Use your large spoon to make small wells in the sauce and crack the eggs into each well. Cover the pan and cook for 5-8 minutes, or until the eggs are done to your liking.

Step 3
Smash the avocado with a fork, add olive oil, salt and black pepper and mix well.

Add the avocado and feta to the top. Garnish with chopped coriander and parsley.

Nutrition Facts	Per Portion (352 g)
Energy	275 kcal
Protein	14g
Carbohydrate	18g
Sugars	9g
Fat	18g
Fatty Acids, Total Saturated	5g
Fibres	8g
Sodium	942mg

Breakfast Burrito

Time: 10 minutes
2 Portions

Ingredients

- 1 tsp Chilli Paste
- 1 Egg
- 1 tsp Olive Oil
- 50g Kale
- 7 Cherry Tomatoes, halved
- 1/2 Avocado, small and sliced
- 1 Wholemeal Tortilla Wrap

Method

Step 1
Whisk the chilli paste with the egg and some seasoning in a jug.

Step 2
Heat the oil in a large frying pan, add the kale and tomatoes. Cook until the kale is wilted and the tomatoes have softened, then push everything to the side of the pan.

Step 3
Pour the beaten egg into the cleared half of the pan and scramble. Layer everything into the centre of your wrap, topping with the avocado, then wrap up and eat immediately.

Nutrition Facts	Per Portion (160 g)
Energy	211 kcal
Protein	7g
Carbohydrate	18g
Sugars	2g
Fat	15g
Fatty Acids, Total Saturated	3g
Fibres	7g
Sodium	374mg

Banana and Oats Bake

Time: 25 minutes
2 Portions

Ingredients

- 1 Banana, very ripe
- 30g Blueberries (optional)
- 30g Jumbo Porridge Oats
- 1 tsp of Cinnamon
- 75ml Milk of your choice, plus extra to serve
- 2 Walnuts, roughly chopped
- 75ml Water

Method

Step 1
Heat oven to 190°C/170°C fan/gas 5.

Step 2
Mash up half a banana, then mix it with the oats, cinnamon, milk, water and a pinch of salt, and pour into a baking dish. Top with the remaining banana halves and scatter over the walnuts.

Step 3
Bake for 20-25 minutes until the oats are creamy and have absorbed most of the liquid. Add the blueberries to serve.

Nutrition Facts	Per Portion (181 g)
Energy	138 kcal
Protein	3g
Carbohydrate	26g
Sugars	9g
Fat	4g
Fatty Acids, Total Saturated	0g
Fibres	4g
Sodium	28mg

Lunch

Healthy Fish and Chips

Time: 40 minutes
3 Portions

Ingredients

- 2 Sea Bass Fillets
- 1 Lemon
- 30g Low-Carb Breadcrumbs
- 180g Carrots
- 150g Peas, fresh
- 1 tbsp Dried Dill
- 200g Sweet Potatoes (optional)
- 30g Cheddar Cheese, finely grated
- Garlic Puree
- Olive Oil

Method

Step 1
Preheat the oven to 220°C. Cut the potatoes into chips and add them to a baking tray. Add a drizzle of olive oil, salt, and pepper, and toss everything to mix well. Put in the oven for about 25 minutes.

Step 2
Grate the carrots.

Mix the breadcrumbs with the dill, cheddar, salt, pepper and ½ tablespoon of olive oil.

Step 3
Once the sweet potatoes are nearly cooked, pat dry the sea bass with kitchen paper. Rub some garlic puree around the fish and add the low-carb breadcrumb onto the fish. Put it to roast for about 12 minutes.

Step 4
While the fish is cooking, sauté the carrots with garlic and olive oil for about 4 minutes. Do exactly the same with the peas.

Now it is just time to assemble – Place the carrots at the bottom, then the fish. The peas are just on the side. I normally serve the sweet potatoes in a side dish.

Nutrition Facts	Per Portion (300 g)
Energy	358 kcal
Protein	24g
Carbohydrate	32g
Sugars	11g
Fat	15g
Fatty Acids, Total Saturated	3g
Fibres	7g
Sodium	334mg

Sea Bass with Rosemary Lentils and Asparagus

Sea Bass with Rosemary Lentils and Asparagus

Time: 25 minutes
2 Portions

Ingredients

- 2 Sea Bass Fillet
- 200g cooked puy lentils
- Rosemary
- 250g asparagus
- 125g cherry tomatoes
- 4 garlic cloves minced
- Garlic Granules

Method

Step 1
Preheat the oven to 220°C. Rub half of the minced garlic, salt, and pepper onto the sea bass. Place one stem of rosemary under each fish (skin-side up) and put it in the oven to roast for about 12 minutes.

Boil a kettle of water.

Step 2
To sauté the puy lentils, just add one tablespoon of olive oil in medium heat. Add the crushed garlic and cook for 1-minute stirring to not burn. Now add the lentils and sauté for about 3 minutes or until it is hot enough.

When they are nearly ready, sprinkle the fresh rosemary over it.

Step 3
Place the asparagus in a pan with a little of the boiled water, just enough to cover it. Cover the pan with a lid and cook it for about 5 minutes (if the asparagus are thin, leave it for about 4 minutes). Once ready, rinse it with cold water to stop the cooking process.

Step 4
Now it is time to sauté them with cherry tomatoes. Add one tablespoon of olive oil to a pan. When hot, add the cherry tomatoes and sauté for one minute, add the asparagus and toss it to mix well. Add salt, pepper, and garlic granules.

Just assemble the dish and serve!

Nutrition Facts	Per Portion (424 g)
Energy	289 kcal
Protein	37g
Carbohydrate	29g
Sugars	6g
Fat	4g
Fatty Acids, Total Saturated	1g
Fibres	12g
Sodium	332mg

Naked Beef Burger

Naked Beef Burger

Time: 35 minutes
3 Portions

Ingredients

- 2 Sweet Potatoes
- 125g Cherry Tomatoes
- 1 Shallot
- 20g Cheddar Cheese
- 2 tsp Balsamic Vinegar
- 1 tbsp Italian Herbs, dried
- 10g Breadcrumbs, gluten-free
- 240g Beef, minced
- 40g Rocket Salad

Method

Step 1
Preheat your oven to 200°C. Chop the sweet potatoes into 2cm wide wedges (no need to peel!). Halve the baby plum tomatoes. Halve, peel, and thinly slice the shallot. Grate the cheddar.

Step 2
Pop the sweet potato wedges on a large low sided wide baking tray. Drizzle with oil, then season with salt and pepper. Toss to coat, then spread out in a single layer. Once your oven is hot, roast on the top shelf of your oven until golden, 25-30 minutes. Turn halfway through cooking.

Step 3
Heat a drizzle of oil in a large frying pan over medium heat. Once hot, add the shallot and season with salt and pepper and cook, stirring regularly, until soft and caramelised, 6-7 minutes. Add half the balsamic vinegar with a pinch of erythritol (if you have some) and cook for 1 minute until the liquid has evaporated and the onions look glossy. Transfer to a small bowl and set aside.

Step 4
Meanwhile, put the dried Italian herb in a large bowl. Add the breadcrumbs and 50ml of water. Season with salt and pepper, mix, then add the beef mince. Mix with your hands until combined, then shape into burgers about 2cm thick, 1 per person.

Step 5

Wipe out the pan used for the shallot, heat a splash of oil over medium heat. Once hot, add the burgers and fry until browned on the outside and cooked through, 12-14 minutes in total. Carefully turn them every 4 minutes and lower the heat if they are burning. When the burgers are cooked, remove the pan from the heat, sprinkle the cheese on the burgers, cover with a lid or foil and leave to rest for a few minutes. The cheese will melt as the burgers rest.

Step 6

Meanwhile, pop the remaining balsamic vinegar and a drizzle of oil into a bowl and season with a pinch of salt and pepper. Mix together, add the tomatoes. When the beef burgers are ready, add the rocket to the dressing, toss to coat. Share the burgers between your plates and top with the caramelised balsamic onions. Serve with sweet potato wedges and rocket salad.

Nutrition Facts	Per Portion (218 g)
Energy	370 kcal
Protein	20g
Carbohydrate	21g
Sugars	7g
Fat	23g
Fatty Acids, Total Saturated	8g
Fibres	3g
Sodium	272mg

Creamy Chicken and Mushrooms Fricassee

Creamy Chicken and Mushrooms Fricassee

Time: 20 minutes
2 Portions

Ingredients

- 250g of Chicken Breast
- 100g of Soft Cheese
- Spring Onions
- 200g Cooked Rice
- 1 tbsp of Shaoxing Wine or Saké or Dry Sherry
- 15ml Red Wine Vinegar
- 100ml Chicken Stock (broth)
- 1 tbsp Dijon Mustard
- 160g Chestnut Mushrooms
- 50g Baby Leaf Salad
- 2 tbsp Olive Oil

Method

Step 1
Boil a kettle. Heat a large, wide-based pan (preferably non-stick) with a drizzle of olive oil over high heat. Meanwhile, combine the red wine vinegar with olive oil and a pinch of salt and pepper - this is your dressing. Slice the mushrooms.

Step 2
Once hot, add the diced chicken and cook for 2 min. Add Dijon mustard to your chicken stock.

Step 3
Add the chestnut mushrooms into the pan with the chicken and cook for a further 1 min. Add the Shaoxing wine and cook for 30 sec further. Add the stock to the pan and bring to a boil over high heat. Add the soft cheese, season with a pinch of salt and pepper and give everything a good mix up. Cook for 1-2 min further or until the chicken is cooked through; this is your chicken & mushroom fricassée.

Step 4
Serve the chicken & mushroom fricassée, rice and baby leaf salad. Garnish the fricassee with the sliced spring onions, drizzle the baby leaf salad with the dressing and let everyone enjoy!

Nutrition Facts	Per Portion (465 g)
Energy	434 kcal
Protein	40g
Carbohydrate	32g
Sugars	6g
Fat	14g
Fatty Acids, Total Saturated	4g
Fibres	3g
Sodium	564mg

Chicken Parisian Style

Chicken Parisian Style

Time: 35 minutes
2 Portions

Ingredients

- 2 Carrots
- 2 Chicken Breasts
- 1 tbsp of Parisian Herbs (white pepper, nutmeg, paprika, clove buds, thyme, cinnamon, basil and bay leaves)
- 1 Red Onion
- 3 Garlic Cloves
- 100ml of Chicken Broth (I use homemade)
- 200g Brown Lentils, already cooked
- 200g Spinach
- 30g Greek Yoghurt (the original recipe was with Crème Fraiche)
- 1 tbsp of Wholegrain Mustard
- Garlic Granules

Method

Step 1
Preheat the oven to 200°C, fill and boil the kettle. Cut the carrot into sticks. Place on a baking sheet. Drizzle with oil, add garlic granules, salt and pepper. Spread to bake and place on the top shelf of your oven until the carrots are golden brown and tender for 20 minutes. Turn halfway.

Step 2
Meanwhile, place the chicken in a bowl with a drizzle of olive oil and Parisian herbs. Season with salt. Rub the seasonings on the chicken. Heat a large skillet over medium-high heat. Brown the chicken for 2-3 minutes on each side. Transfer to the roasting pan with the carrots and bake on the top shelf of the oven for 18-20 minutes.

Step 3
Meanwhile, peel and finely slice the red onion. Peel and grate the garlic.

Clean the now-empty skillet and return to medium heat. Add a little olive oil and the red onion. Stir and cook until tender, 5-6 minutes, then add the garlic. Cook for another minute and then add the chicken broth. Bring to a boil, then lower a little and bring to a boil to cut in half, 5-6 minutes. When ready, remove the lentils from the heat and add the yoghurt (or Crème Fraiche) and mustard.

Step 4
Now it's time to sauté the spinach with the garlic - just a drizzle of olive oil. As soon as it is reduced in size, remove the water and add the garlic. Sauté for 1 minute, and it's ready.

Step 5
When the chicken is cooked, take it out of the oven and let it rest for a few minutes on a cutting board. Cut each breast into slices.

Nutrition Facts	Per Portion (490 g)
Energy	352 kcal
Protein	42g
Carbohydrate	36g
Sugars	8g
Fat	6g
Fatty Acids, Total Saturated	2g
Fibres	5g
Sodium	916mg

Quick Tuna Salad

Time: 15 minutes
1 Portion

Ingredients

- 1 Tuna (130g), tinned
- 100g Green Beans
- 70g Cannellini Beans, already cooked
- 1 tbsp Capers
- 8 Cherry Tomatoes
- Red Onion
- Lemon
- 1 tbsp Olive Oil
- Lettuce

Method

Step 1
Finely slice the red onion.

Halve the cherry tomatoes.

Drain the tuna and the capers.

Trim the green beans.

Step 2
Cook the green beans covered for about 5 min with a little water. Once ready, add cold water to maintain the bright colour and stop the cooking process.

Step 3
Add the cannellini beans, tuna, onions, cherry tomatoes, capers, olive oil and lemon juice to a bowl and give a good mix. Then serve with the lettuce and use the caper berries to decorate.

Nutrition Facts	Per Portion (500 g)
Energy	454 kcal
Protein	42g
Carbohydrate	27g
Sugars	8g
Fat	20g
Fatty Acids, Total Saturated	3g
Fibres	9g
Sodium	926mg

Mediterranean Sea Bass

Mediterranean Sea Bass

Time: 35 minutes
2 Portions

Ingredients

- 1 Aubergine, small
- 1 Courgette
- 125g Cherry Tomatoes
- 2 Red Onions
- 50ml Vegetable Stock
- 1 tbsp Tomato Puree
- 20g Breadcrumbs,
  gluten-free
- 10g Basil
- 20g Cheddar Cheese,
  grated
- 2 Sea Bass Fillets

Method

Step 1
Preheat the oven to 220°C.

Peel and chop the red onions roughly. Top, tail and chop the courgette roughly into bite-sized pieces. Chop the cherry tomatoes in half. Grate the cheddar cheese into a bowl. Add the gluten-free breadcrumbs and season generously with salt and pepper. Add a drizzle of vegetable oil and give everything a good stir - this is your cheesy breadcrumb mixture.

Step 2
Pat the Sea Bass, fillets dry with kitchen paper and add them to a baking tray (use the tin to avoid a mess). Sprinkle the cheesy breadcrumb mixture over the fillets until they're totally covered. Put the tray in the oven for 10-15 min or until the cheesy breadcrumb mixture is starting to turn golden and the fish is cooked - this is your cheesy baked fish.

Step 3
While the fish is cooking, heat a large, wide-based pan (preferably non - stick) with a drizzle of olive oil over medium heat. Once hot, add the chopped onion, courgette and tomato paste and cook for 2-3 min or until starting to soften.

Add the cherry tomatoes and cook for 4-5 min further or until all the vegetables have softened. Add the vegetable stock and cook for 1-2 min further. Season generously with salt and pepper - these are your Mediterranean vegetables.

Once done, tear the basil leaves into your Mediterranean vegetables and serve with the cheesy baked fish.

Nutrition Facts	Per Portion (449 g)
Energy	270 kcal
Protein	31g
Carbohydrate	18g
Sugars	10g
Fat	8g
Fatty Acids, Total Saturated	3g
Fibres	3g
Sodium	268mg

Herby Crispy Skin Roasted Chicken

Herby Crispy Skin Roasted Chicken

Time: 50 minutes
2 Portions

Ingredients

- 200g Chicken Breast Fillets
- 160g Green Beans
- 125g Cherry Tomatoes
- 350g Potatoes
- 50g Soft Cheese
- 5 Garlic Cloves, grated
- 1 tbsp Oregano
- 1 tsp Butter
- 1 tsp Olive Oil
- Salt and Pepper

Method

Step 1
Preheat the oven to 220°C. Boil a kettle. Peel and grate the garlic. Add half of the grated garlic to a bowl with the soft cheese, half of the dried oregano (save the rest for later!) and a pinch of black pepper - this is your garlic & herb mixture.

Step 2
Slice a lengthwise incision into each chicken breast but don't cut all the way, though (this will provide a pocket for the stuffing!). Stuff each chicken breast with the garlic & herb mixture.

Add the stuffed chicken to a small ovenproof dish and scatter over the cherry tomatoes.

Drizzle with olive oil and sprinkle with the remaining dried oregano and a pinch of salt and pepper. Add the dish to the oven for 20-25 min or until the chicken is cooked through (no pink meat!). The tomatoes and garlic & herb mixture have created a sauce in the bottom of the dish.

Step 3
While the chicken is cooking, peel the potatoes, then cut them into small bite-sized pieces. Add the chopped potatoes to a pot of boiled water with a pinch of salt over high heat and cook for 10-12 min or until fork-tender. Once cooked, drain and return to the pot to steam dry.

Step 4
Add a drizzle of olive oil to a pan. Once it is hot, add the green beans and sauté for about 5 min. Add in the remaining garlic and sauté for another minute. Add a splash of water and let it cook for another 2 -3 minutes covered. Season with salt and pepper.

Step 5
Return the drained potatoes to low heat and add a knob of butter. Season with a pinch of salt and pepper and mash until smooth.

Step 6
Serve the garlic & herb stuffed chicken over the mashed potatoes. Spoon over the cherry tomatoes and sauce from the dish and serve the green beans to the side.

Nutrition Facts	Per Portion (453 g)
Energy	351 kcal
Protein	31g
Carbohydrate	35g
Sugars	7g
Fat	10g
Fatty Acids, Total Saturated	4g
Fibres	8g
Sodium	537mg

Chicken with a Low Carb Crust balsamic Green Beans

Chicken with a Low Carb Crust and Balsamic Green Beans

Time: 45 minutes
2 Portions

Ingredients

- 200g Green Beans
- 2 Garlic Cloves
- 1 bunch of Parsley
- 1 tbsp of Provencal Herbs (thyme, basil, rosemary, tarragon, savoury, marjoram, oregano and bay leaf all dry)
- 10g Low-Carb Breadcrumbs
- 2 tbsp Olive Oil
- 2 Chicken Breast
- 1 tsp Mayonnaise
- 1 tbsp Balsamic
- 75ml Water for the beans

Method

Step 1
Trim the green beans. Peel and mince the garlic (or use the garlic press).

Meanwhile, roughly chop the parsley (stalks and all). Put half the parsley in a small bowl and mix in the breadcrumbs, Provencale herbs, olive oil (see ingredients for amount) and season with salt. Pop the chicken breasts on a baking tray and season with salt and black pepper. Using the back of a spoon, spread the mayo over the top half of each breast and then sprinkle over the crumb mixture. Roast the chicken on the top shelf of your oven until cooked through and golden on top, 25-30 minutes.

Step 2
Heat a splash of oil in your frying pan on high heat. Stir-fry the green beans for 2 minutes. Add the garlic and season with salt. Add the water. Pop a lid on the pan and steam until just tender, 3-5 minutes. Drain any leftover water, then stir through and olive oil.

Step 3
Time to serve - just add the chicken to a plate and place some garlicky green beans alongside. Drizzle the balsamic dressing from the beans around the plate and finish with a sprinkling of the remaining parsley.

Low-Carb Breadcrumbs

Take the low-carb/gluten-free bread and cut it into very small 1cm pieces, and place in the oven to bake for 45min to 60min. When ready, let it cool for about 5 minutes. Place in the processor until very thin. Place into an airtight container and store at room temperature for up to two weeks.

Nutrition Facts	Per Portion (231 g)
Energy	358 kcal
Protein	35g
Carbohydrate	7g
Sugars	3g
Fat	21g
Fatty Acids, Total Saturated	3g
Fibres	2g
Sodium	78mg

Dinner

Soy Ginger Salmon

Soy Ginger Salmon

Time: 35 minutes
2 Portions

Ingredients

- 2 Salmon Fillets
- 200g Carrots
- 100g Broccoli
- 100g Green Beans
- 2 tbsp Toasted Sesame Seeds
- 1 tbsp Ginger, crushed
- 3 tbsp Low Sodium Soy Sauce
- 1 tbsp Rice Vinegar
- 4 cloves Garlic, crushed
- 2 tbsp Olive Oil
- 1/2 tbsp Chilli Paste (optional)
- 1 tbsp Erythritol Syrup

Method

Step 1

Place a rack in the centre of your oven and preheat to 220°C. Place a large cast-iron skillet or other sturdy, ovenproof skillet on a burner set to high and heat for at least 10 minutes. You want the pan screaming hot, or the salmon will stick to it.

Step 2

In a small saucepan, stir together the soy sauce, rice vinegar, garlic, and ginger. Bring to a simmer over medium-high, then remove from heat and stir in the syrup and chilli paste (if used). Remove a few spoonfuls spoonsful of the cooked glaze in a separate bowl for serving.

Step 3

Drizzle the salmon with olive oil and brush so that it is evenly coated. Place the salmon skin-side up on the hot skillet. Let cook for about 3 minutes, totally undisturbed, until the salmon forms a nice crust. When the salmon turns opaque on the sides and starts to turn opaque on top, use a flexible spatula to flip the salmon so that it is skin-side down. Brush or spoon the remaining glaze in the saucepan all over the top. Place the skillet immediately into the oven and let cook for 6 minutes (the salmon will appear a little undercooked in the centre but will finish cooking as it rests).

Remove from the oven and cover with foil. Let rest for 4 to 5 minutes. Serve immediately, topped with reserved glaze and sesame seeds.

Step 4

For the vegetables, simply add a tablespoon of olive oil to the pan on medium heat and put in the carrots, broccoli and green beans for about 4 minutes, then add garlic and cook it for another 1 minute.

Add two tablespoon of water to the pan and cover it to cook for another 2-4 minutes. Season it with a little lemon, salt, pepper and chilli if you like.

Nutrition Facts	Per Portion (370 g)
Energy	382 kcal
Protein	28g
Carbohydrate	32g
Sugars	8g
Fat	21g
Fatty Acids, Total Saturated	3g
Fibres	8g
Sodium	991mg

Beef and Mushrooms Casserole

Time: 45 minutes
4 Portions

Ingredients

- 400g of Beef, cut into strips
- 2 Onions
- 4 Garlic Cloves
- 400ml of Beef Broth
- 1/2 tbsp Wholemeal Flour
- 300ml of Red Wine
- 1 Bay Leaf
- Rosemary
- 150g of Fresh Sliced Mushrooms (Shiitake or Cremini mushrooms work well)
- 2 tbs of Dijon Mustard
- Salt and Pepper
- Olive Oil
- Parsley, chopped

Method

Step 1
Heat a drizzle of olive oil in a deep pan and seal all the pieces of meat. Remove the meat from the pan and add the onions, chopped garlic and bay leaf. When the onions are soft, drizzle with the broth and bring to a boil.

Step 2
Now, dissolve the wholemeal flour in the red wine and add to the pan. Stir well to avoid lumps. Add the meat and a little pepper, a little salt and simmer for 20 minutes.

Step 3
After that time, check the beef. If it is still hard, let it cook a little longer. If the meat is already soft, add the sliced mushrooms and cook for another 20 minutes.

To finish, add the Dijon mustard that will give it a spicy touch, a little rosemary and more seasoning if needed. Sprinkle with chopped parsley and serve with sautéed vegetables.

Nutrition Facts	Per Portion (350g)
Energy	324 kcal
Protein	29g
Carbohydrate	15g
Sugars	5g
Fat	10g
Fatty Acids, Total Saturated	4g
Fibres	2g
Sodium	530mg

Cod with Lemon and Capers Sauce

Cod with Lemon and Capers Sauce

Time: 35 minutes
2 Portions

Ingredients

- 300g Cod, fresh
- Salt and Pepper
- 200g Courgettes
- 150g Cherry Tomatoes
- 2 tbsp Capers
- 2 tbsp Butter
- 4 Garlic Cloves, minced
- 1 Lemon
- 2 tbsp Parsley
- Garlic Granules

Method

Step 1
Preheat the oven to 220°C. Add the cod into separate pieces of foil paper with a little olive oil, lemon, salt, pepper and garlic granules. Put it to roast for 15 min.

Step 2
Slice the courgettes and half the cherry tomatoes. Mince the garlic. Finely chop the parsley.

Step 3
5 min before the fish is ready, sauté the courgettes with a drizzle of olive oil and half of the garlic for about 5 min. When the courgettes are nearly ready, add the cherry tomatoes and sauté for another minute.

Step 4
Place the vegetables on a plate and add the cod on top. Then add the sauce all over the dish and sprinkle some parsley to garnish.

Sauce

1. Drain and rinse the capers. If they are large, chop them coarsely.
2. Melt the butter in a small skillet or sauté pan over low heat. Add the minced garlic, lemon juice, lemon zest, and capers. Bring to a simmer and continue cooking over low heat for about 30 seconds.
3. Add the chopped fresh parsley, stir and remove from the heat.
4. Drizzle the warm sauce on overcooked fish, chicken, or turkey cutlets, and serve immediately.

Nutrition Facts	Per Portion (347 g)
Energy	231 kcal
Protein	30g
Carbohydrate	7g
Sugars	5g
Fat	10g
Fatty Acids, Total Saturated	6g
Fibres	2g
Sodium	1328mg

Stuffed Aubergine Italian Style

Stuffed Aubergine Italian Style

Time: 1 hour
3 Portions

Ingredients

- 2 (500g each) Aubergines
- Olive Oil Cooking Spray
- Basil Leaves (handful), shredded
- 50g Parmesan, grated
- Basil Leaves, small and fresh for serving

Filling

- 1 tbsp Olive Oil
- 1 Brown Onion, medium and finely chopped
- 3 Garlic Cloves, minced
- 1 Carrot, small and finely chopped
- 1 Celery Stalk, finely chopped
- 400g Beef, minced
- 1x400g Canned Tomatoes, chopped
- 3/4 cup Beef Stock
- 1 tbsp Tomato Paste
- 1 tsp Oregano, dried

Method

Step 1
Preheat the oven to 200°C. Line a baking tray with baking paper. Pierce aubergine several times with a fork. Spray all over with oil. Place on a prepared tray. Bake for 40 minutes or until tender. Once ready, let it cool slightly.

Step 2
Make the Beef
Heat oil in a large saucepan over medium heat. Add onion, garlic, carrot and celery. Cook, stirring, for 5 minutes or until the onion has softened. Add the minced beef. Cook, stirring with a wooden spoon to break up mince, for 5 minutes or until browned.
Add tomatoes, stock, oregano and paste. Bring to the boil. Reduce heat to low. Simmer, covered, for 30 minutes. Remove the cover. Simmer for 20 to 25 minutes or until thickened.

Step 3
Cut aubergines in half lengthwise. Using a spoon, scoop flesh from the aubergine halves, leaving a 1cm border. Finely chop.

Combine the beef, shredded basil and chopped aubergine in a medium bowl. Place aubergine halves on a baking tray. Spoon beef mixture into the aubergine. Sprinkle with parmesan. Bake for 20 minutes or until heated through. Serve sprinkled with basil leaves.

Nutrition Facts	Per Portion (696 g)
Energy	412 kcal
Protein	44g
Carbohydrate	18g
Sugars	15g
Fat	18g
Fatty Acids, Total Saturated	8g
Fibres	3g
Sodium	539mg

Roasted Beef with Madeira Sauce

Roasted Beef with Madeira Sauce

Time: 45 minutes
2 Portions

Ingredients

- 230g Steak of your choice
- 200g Carrots
- 6 Garlic Cloves
- 250g Mushrooms
- Parsley
- Olive Oil
- Rosemary
- Salt and Pepper

Method

Step 1
Allow the steak to stay at room temperature for about 30 minutes before you cook. This will help to obtain final internal pressure easily. Preheat the oven to 250°C. Chop the carrots in julienne and slice the mushrooms finely. Mince the garlic.

Step 2
Pan-fry the steak with very little olive oil for about 2 minutes on each side. Then place in the oven with rosemary under the steaks for about 8-10 minutes. Remove it and let it rest for a few minutes before serving.

Step 3
Sauté the carrots with 1/3 of the garlic for about 5 minutes or until it reaches your favourite consistency.

Step 4
Now sauté the mushrooms again in a drizzle of olive oil with the remaining garlic for about 5 minutes, then reduce the heat and let it simmer for another 5 minutes. Add parsley.

Step 5
Once it is all ready, just assemble the dish by placing the mushrooms on the plate first. Then place the steak just above it. The carrots would go on the side. To finish the dish, add the Madeira sauce on top of the beef.

Step 6
The Sauce

- 1 tbsp of Butter
- Onion, chopped
- 1 Garlic Clove, minced
- 2 tbsp of Wholewheat Flour
- 50ml of Dry Red Wine
- 250ml of Broth
- Salt to taste
- Black Pepper to taste

Preparation:
1. In a pan, over medium heat, melt the butter and then sauté the onion and garlic.
2. As soon as the onion wilts, add the flour little by little and mix without stopping.
3. Then add the wine and mix well.
4. Add the broth, salt and pepper.
5. Mix well until the flour dissolves well and the sauce is full-bodied.
6. After the sauce is full-bodied, turn off the heat and sift it to remove the pieces of onion and garlic.
7. Bring the sauce back to low heat until it reaches the perfect consistency.

Nutrition Facts	Per Portion (339 g)
Energy	317 kcal
Protein	27g
Carbohydrate	12g
Sugars	5g
Fat	19g
Fatty Acids, Total Saturated	5g
Fibres	4g
Sodium	1108mg

Smoked Salmon and Avocado Salad

Time: 10 minutes
2 Portions

Ingredients

- 200g Smoked Salmon
- 1 Avocado
- Rocket Salad, 2 handfuls
- 2 tbsp Capers
- 2 tbsp Olive Oil
- 1 Lemon
- Salt
- Black Pepper

Method

Place the smoked salmon directly onto the plate you will be serving.

Then add the rocket in the middle of the plate, just above the salmon. Add half avocado sliced (on each plate) onto the rocket. Sprinkle the capers over the salmon.

Mix the olive oil, salt and lemon juice. Drizzle all over the dish. Sprinkle the black pepper.

Nutrition Facts	Per Portion (218 g)
Energy	400 kcal
Protein	25g
Carbohydrate	8g
Sugars	1g
Fat	31g
Fatty Acids, Total Saturated	5g
Fibres	5g
Sodium	1490mg

Summer Roast Chicken Salad

Summer Roast Chicken Salad

Ingredients

- 125g Cherry Tomatoes
- 50g Rocket Salad
- 80g Green Beans, trimmed
- 1 tsp Basil, dried
- 5g Dijon Mustard
- 15ml Cider Vinegar
- 2x125g Chicken Breast
- 2 tbsp Olive Oil

Method

Step 1
Preheat the oven to 200°C.

Add the chicken breasts to a baking tray with a drizzle of olive oil and a generous pinch of salt and pepper. Put the tray in the oven for an initial 10 min.

Step 2
Meanwhile, chop the cherry tomatoes in half. Add the chopped tomatoes to a bowl with the dried basil, 1 tablespoon olive oil and a generous pinch of salt and pepper.

Once the chicken has been in the oven for 10 min, remove the tray from the oven and surround it with tomatoes. Return the tray to the oven for a further 12-15 min or until the chicken is cooked through (no pink meat!) and the juices run clear.

Step 3
Whilst the chicken is cooking, combine the Dijon mustard and cider vinegar with 1 tablespoon olive oil, 1 teaspoon erythritol and a pinch of salt and pepper. Mix everything together - this is your dressing.

Step 4
Boil a kettle. Add the green beans to a pot, cover them with boiled water (just enough to cover them) with a pinch of salt. Bring to the boil over high heat and cook for 3-4 minutes. Drain then set aside.

Step 5
Once the chicken is cooked, serve it with the rocket and tomatoes on plates and top with the green beans. Drizzle over the dressing and season with a crack of black pepper.

Nutrition Facts	Per Portion (276 g)
Energy	284 kcal
Protein	31g
Carbohydrate	4g
Sugars	3g
Fat	15g
Fatty Acids, Total Saturated	2g
Fibres	3g
Sodium	185mg

Tuna Tartare

Time: 30 minutes
3 Portions

Ingredients

- 200g of Tuna, skinless and fresh
- 1 tbsp of Dijon Mustard
- 4 Anchovy Fillets, chopped
- 1 tbsp Red Chillies, finely chopped (remove the seeds)
- 2 tbsp Olive Oil (I used part of anchovy oil)
- 2 tbsp Lemon Juice
- 2 tbsp Capers, rinsed and chopped
- 1 tbsp Parsley, chopped
- Red Onion, chopped
- Salt and Pepper to taste
- 1 Avocado
- Caper Berries for garnish

Method

Step 1
Combine the Dijon, the anchovy and the chillies in a large bowl. Add the olive oil, constantly stirring, until emulsified. Add the lemon juice. Add the capers, parsley and onion and mix well.

Step 2
Cut the tuna into very small pieces. Add the tuna to the vinaigrette and stir until the fish absorbs the sauce. Season with salt and pepper to taste. Cut the avocado into very small pieces, season with olive oil and salt.

Step 3
Now just assemble (avocado at the bottom), then tuna and serve with caper berries on top.

Nutrition Facts	Per Portion (271 g)
Energy	364 kcal
Protein	32g
Carbohydrate	8g
Sugars	2g
Fat	23g
Fatty Acids, Total Saturated	4g
Fibres	4g
Sodium	1061mg

Stir Fried Prawns Chinese Style

Time: 20 minutes
2 Portions

Ingredients

- 400g Whole King Prawns, peeled
- 4 Garlic Gloves, peeled and minced
- 1 Red Chilli, deseeded or flakes
- 3 Shallots, peeled
- 1 Spring Onion
- 1 tbsp Olive Oil
- 150g Green Beans
- 150g Broccoli Spears
- 1 tbsp Toasted Sesame Seeds
- 2 tbsp Premium Oyster Sauce
- 1 tbsp Soy Sauce

Method

Step 1
If using frozen prawns, defrost the king prawns by submerging them in cold water.

Combine the Premium Oyster Sauce & Soy Sauce to marinade with the king prawns.

Step 2
Grate the garlic. Chop the chilli, finely slice the shallots and spring onion. Trim the green beans.

Step 3
Heat the oil in a wok or frying pan on high heat. Add the garlic and three-quarters of the chilli and shallots.

Stir-fry for 1 to 2 minutes.

Add the vegetables and stir fry for about 3 minutes. Add the king prawns and stir-fry for another 4 to 5 minutes.

Step 4
Sprinkle the remaining chilli, sesame seeds, spring onion and tomatoes. Serve immediately.

Nutrition Facts	Per Portion (499 g)
Energy	330 kcal
Protein	45g
Carbohydrate	16g
Sugars	5g
Fat	11g
Fatty Acids, Total Saturated	2g
Fibres	7g
Sodium	1455mg

Pumpkin and Chicken Soup

Time: 50 minutes
3 Portions

Ingredients

- 600g Chicken Breast
- 1 1/2 tsp Salt
- 400g Pumpkin
- 1 Onion
- 4 Garlic Cloves
- 200ml Chicken Stock
- Parsley, dried
- Spring Onions
- Chilli Flakes

Method

Step 1
Dice the onions finely. Finely slice the spring onions.

Chop the pumpkin into about 2cm pieces. Put it in a pan with the chicken stock and a little more water to boil. When it reaches boiling point, reduce to low heat for about 30 minutes.

Step 2
In the meantime, brown the chicken in a pan with a drizzle of olive oil, add the onion, garlic, dried parsley and salt. Pull the chicken in very fine pieces. Once the chicken is cooked, pull the chicken.

Step 3
Place the soup in a food processor or blender until it becomes creamy. Then, put the soup back into a pan with the chicken and let it simmer for about 20 minutes uncovered.

Serve the soup and garnish it with spring onions and chilli flakes.

Nutrition Facts	Per Portion (443 g)
Energy	316 kcal
Protein	49g
Carbohydrate	15g
Sugars	6g
Fat	6g
Fatty Acids, Total Saturated	1g
Fibres	2g
Sodium	1278mg

Pork Fillet with Red Wine Sauce

Pork Fillet with Red Wine Sauce

Time: 1 hour
4 portions

Ingredientes

- 400g Pork Fillet (for the person on a diet, the consumption should be 80g cooked)
- 160g Kale
- 160g Carrots
- 2 Red Onions
- Garlic Powder
- 3 tbsp Olive Oil
- Thyme
- 30g Butter
- 1 Red Onion, medium and finely chopped
- 1 Garlic Clove, crushed
- 1/2 cup Dry Red Wine
- 1 cup Beef Broth
- 4 slices of parma ham

Method:

Step 1

Kale: Put a drizzle of oil in the sauté, add a little water and cover the pan. Let it cook for about three minutes. Add salt, black pepper and crushed garlic and sauté for another 2-3 minutes.

Step 2

Roasted vegetables: simply place the vegetables together in a roasting pan, make sure the sizes of the pieces are uniform. Add a spoonful of olive oil, garlic powder, salt, black pepper and thyme and mix everything. Bake at 200°C for about 20 minutes.

Step 3

To get the best pork loin, dry the pork and season with salt and pepper.

Before roasting, we always seal the pork from all sides first. After seasoning, place in a hot pan. Seal all sides until golden. It's okay if the pork is still raw in the middle.

When the pork is golden on all sides, it is ready to go to the oven. Add rosemary and wrap in the prosciutto.

To finish cooking the pork, just put it in the hot oven. We keep the oven temperature around 250 degrees and roast the pork for 15 to 20 minutes.

Step 4

Red Wine Sauce

Melt the butter in a skillet over medium heat. Add the onion. Cook for 3 to 4 minutes or until tender. Add the garlic. Cook, stirring, for 1 minute or until fragrant.

Add the wine. Let it boil. Reduce the heat to medium-low. Cook for 3 to 5 minutes. Add broth. Let it boil. Reduce the heat to medium. Cook for 10 to 12 minutes or until thickened.

Nutrition Facts	Per Portion (226 G)
Energy	357 kcal
Protein	28g
Carbohydrate	14g
Sugars	6g
Fat	20g
Fatty Acids, Total Saturated	6g
Fibres	4g
Sodium	411mg

Pan Fried Pork with Apple Reduction

Pan Fried Pork with Apple Reduction

Time: 25 minutos
2 Portions

Ingredientes

- 1 bunch of Parsley
- Spring Onions
- 2 Pork Loin Steaks
- 250g Cavolo Nero
- 2 Garlic Cloves, minced
- 75ml Chicken Stock (broth homemade)
- 1 Apple, very ripe
- 1 tsp Cider Vinegar
- 20g Butter

Method:

Step 1
Chop the parsley, including stalks. Finely slice the spring onion. Mince the garlic.

Step 2
Heat a splash of oil in a frying pan over medium-high heat. Season the pork with salt and pepper. Lay the pork in the pan and brown for 2 minutes on each side, then lower the heat to medium and cook for another 8 minutes. Turn every 2 minutes. When the pork is cooked, remove it from the pan and wrap it in foil to rest and keep warm.

Step 3
The apple reduction is done by simply cutting the apple into very small pieces, adding the butter and the cider vinegar to cook in high heat. When it starts to boil, lower the heat and let it simmer for about 15min or until the apple is soft. Mash everything and pass it through a sieve.

Step 4
For the kale, add a tablespoon of olive oil to a pan and sauté for about 2 minutes. Add a splash of water and cook it covered for about 2-3 minutes. Add some grated garlic and cook for another 1 min.

Step 5
When the pork is out of the pan, add the chicken stock. Mix in the apple reduction and parsley. Bring to boil. Stir well, let it simmer for about 5min, then remove from the heat.

Step 6
Serve the kale onto your plates. Slice the pork thinly and arrange on top. Pour any pork juices from the foil parcel into the glaze, reheat thoroughly, then spoon on top of the pork and around the plate.

Nutrition Facts	Per Portion (350g)
Energy	396 kcal
Protein	30g
Carbohydrate	18g
Sugars	10g
Fat	32g
Fatty Acids, Total Saturated	11g
Fibres	7g
Sodium	6302mg

Vegetarian

Melanzana alla Parmigiana

Melanzana alla Parmigiana

Time: 1 hour and 30 minutes
6 Portions

Ingredients

- 2 tbsp Olive Oil, plus extra for brushing
- 3 Garlic Cloves, minced
- 1 Onion, finely chopped
- 3 Thyme Sprigs
- 8 Sage Leaves, large and finely chopped
- 1 tbsp Oregano
- 2x400g Canned Tomatoes, chopped
- 3 tbsp Red Wine Vinegar
- 3 tsp Erythritol
- 3 Aubergines, large and sliced lengthwise as thinly as you can
- 100g Parmesan Cheese, finely grated
- 40g Low-Carb Breadcrumbs
- 50g Pine Nuts
- 150g Mozzarella Cheese, torn into small chunks
- Basil Leaves (handful)

Method

Step 1
Preheat the oven to 200°C.
Heat the oil in a large frying pan (or wide saucepan), add the onion, garlic, oregano, thyme and sage, and cook gently for a few minutes. Tip in the tomatoes, vinegar and erythritol, and gently simmer for 20 minutes until thickened a little.

Step 2
Meanwhile, heat a griddle (or frying) pan. Brush the aubergine slices on both sides with olive oil, then griddle in batches. Each slice should be softened and slightly charred, so don't have the heat too high, or the aubergine will char before softening. Remove to a plate as you go.

Step 3
In a large baking dish, spread a little of the tomato sauce over the base. Mix 25g of the parmesan with the breadcrumbs and pine nuts, and set aside.

Top the sauce with a layer or two of aubergine slices, then season well.

Spoon over a bit more sauce, then scatter over some mozzarella, parmesan and basil leaves. Repeat, layering up – and finish with the last of the tomato sauce.

Scatter over the cheesy breadcrumbs and chill for up to 24 hrs, or bake straight away.

Step 4
Bake for 30-40 minutes until the top is crisp and golden and the tomato sauce is bubbling. Rest for 10 minutes, then scatter with basil leaves and serve with salad.

Nutrition Facts	Per Portion (358 g)
Energy	291 kcal
Protein	15g
Carbohydrate	19g
Sugars	8g
Fat	18g
Fatty Acids, Total Saturated	7g
Fibres	3g
Sodium	309mg

Stuffed Mushrooms with Lentils

Stuffed Mushrooms with Lentils

Time: 20 minutes
2 Portions

Ingredients

- 1 Shallot
- 4 Garlic Cloves
- 40g Cheddar Cheese, grated
- 125g Cherry Tomatoes
- 50g Rocket Salad
- 1 tsp Basil, dried
- 15g Pumpkin Seeds
- 50g Soft Cheese
- 15ml Cider Vinegar
- 200g Green Lentils, cooked
- 300g Portobello Mushrooms

Method

Step 1
Preheat the oven to 220°C.

Add the portobello mushrooms to a baking tray, stems facing up (use tin foil to avoid mess!), with a drizzle of olive oil and a generous pinch of salt and pepper.

Put the tray in the oven for 10 min or until the mushrooms have softened.

While the mushrooms are cooking, peel and finely slice the shallot. Peel and finely chop (or grate) the garlic.

Step 2
Heat a separate large, wide-based pan (preferably non-stick) with a drizzle of olive oil over medium-high heat.

Once hot, add the chopped garlic and sliced shallot with a pinch of salt and cook for 1-2 min or until slightly softened.

Whilst softening, chop the cherry tomatoes in half.

Then add the halved cherry tomatoes to the pan and cook for a further 2-3 min.

Step 3
Add the green lentils, dried basil, soft cheese and half of the cider vinegar (you'll use the rest later) to a pan. Give everything a good mix up and cook for 1-2 min or until the mixture has slightly thickened.

Season with a generous crack of black pepper and a pinch of salt - this is your creamy lentil & tomato filling.

Step 4

Remove the mushrooms from the oven. Don't forget to get rid of any excess mushroom liquid. Add the creamy lentil & tomato filling to the mushrooms and sprinkle the grated cheddar cheese over the top.

Return the stuffed mushrooms to the oven for 10 min or until the cheese has melted.

Step 5

While the stuffed mushrooms are in the oven, combine the remaining cider vinegar, olive oil and a pinch of salt and pepper - this is your dressing.

Now serve the cheesy lentil & tomato stuffed portobellos with the rocket to the side.

Drizzle the rocket with the dressing and sprinkle over the pumpkin seeds.

Nutrition Facts	Per Portion (308 g)
Energy	367 kcal
Protein	26g
Carbohydrate	31g
Sugars	7g
Fat	17g
Fatty Acids, Total Saturated	8g
Fibres	3g
Sodium	261mg

Mushrooms, Spinach and Cheese Quesadilla

Time: 20 minutes
2 Portions

Ingredients

- 1 tbsp Olive Oil
- 60g Mushrooms, sliced
- 2 Garlic Cloves
- 100g Spinach
- Salt to taste
- Pepper to taste
- 3 Eggs
- 2 Wholemeal Tortillas or if you can get a Low-Carb Protein Tortilla
- 70g Mozzarella Cheese, shredded and double for 2 quesadillas
- 30g Parmesan Cheese, shredded and double for 2 quesadillas
- Parsley

Method

Step 1
Let the oil heat up in the skillet and add the mushrooms followed by the garlic. Cook until the mushrooms have softened and caramelised a bit.

Add the spinach and cook until spinach has wilted. Crack in the eggs and scramble with the veggies. Season with salt and pepper, and stir until fully cooked. Remove from the pan and set aside.

Step 2
Place the tortilla in the skillet and add a layer of both kinds of cheese on half of the tortilla.

Add the scramble, top with more cheese and fold the tortilla in half.

Cook for 6 minutes over medium heat, flipping halfway. Serve with salsa and garnish with fresh parsley.

Nutrition Facts	Per Portion (277 g)
Energy	542 kcal
Protein	35g
Carbohydrate	22g
Sugars	2g
Fat	35g
Fatty Acids, Total Saturated	18g
Fibres	6g
Sodium	1184mg

Mushrooms and Black Beans Burger

Mushrooms and Black Beans Burger

Time: 1 hour and 30 minutes
4 Portions

Ingredients

- 200g Portobello mushrooms, cubed in smaller pieces
- 300g Black Beans, rinsed and divided
- 100g Broccoli, fresh and minced
- 200g Red Onion, minced
- 3 Eggs, extra-large and beaten
- 50g Panko or Gluten-Free Panko
- 1 tbsp Worcestershire Sauce
- 2 Garlic Cloves, minced
- 80g Parmesan, fresh and grated
- Olive Oil

Method

Step 1
Finely chop the mushrooms and sauté with a drizzle of olive oil.

Step 2
In a large bowl, add the black beans and mash with a masher (chunks are okay).

Next, add in the mushrooms, broccoli, garlic, onion, Worcestershire and seasoning. Mix just until coated.

Add in the eggs, cheese and breadcrumbs and mix gently with a large spoon until the mixture is combined.

Set aside while you place a medium non-stick pan over medium heat and add in 2 tablespoon of oil.

Step 3
Once the oil starts to heat (about a minute or two), using dampened hands (the mixture will stick to you if you don't), scoop some of the mixtures into the palm of your hand and gently shape into a burger, all the while pressing together. The mixture should hold a burger shape. If it doesn't, add just a tablespoon of more breadcrumbs.

Step 4
Place in the oil and cook for 3-5 minutes per side or until golden brown and a crust has formed on each side. Serve with guacamole (it is yummy!) or steak sauce.

If you are eating during lunchtime, you can have two slices of light low-carb bread.

Nutrition Facts	Per Portion (227 g)
Energy	334 kcal
Protein	23g
Carbohydrate	37g
Sugars	4g
Fat	11g
Fatty Acids, Total Saturated	5g
Fibres	2g
Sodium	224mg

Pesto Butter Beans Salad

Time: 40 minutes
3 Portions

Ingredients

- 1x400g Canned Butter Beans, drained
- 3 Roasted Garlic Cloves
- 70g Pine Nuts
- Juice of 1 Lemon
- 25g Basil
- 3 tbsp of Olive Oil
- Dash of Water
- 100g Frozen Peas
- Spinach, 2 large handfuls
- Pinch of Salt

Method

Step 1
Put your garlic wrapped in foil paper with a drizzle of olive oil to roast for about 20 minutes.

Place the roasted garlic, pine nuts, lemon juice, basil, olive oil, a pinch of salt and a dash of water into a blender and blend until a slightly chunky pesto forms.

Step 2
Place a pan over medium heat and add a drizzle of olive oil. Once warm, add the butter beans and cook for 5 minutes until they crisp up around the edges.

Step 3
At this point, add the peas and spinach and cook for 5-10 minutes until everything has warmed through and the spinach has wilted. Once finished and off the heat, add in the pesto.

Nutrition Facts	Per Portion (235 g)
Energy	392 kcal
Protein	14g
Carbohydrate	23g
Sugars	4g
Fat	28g
Fatty Acids, Total Saturated	3g
Fibres	2g
Sodium	668mg

Warm Spring Salad

Warm Spring Salad

Time: 35 minutes
2 Portions

Ingredients

- 150g Peas
- 150g Broad Beans
- 2 Courgettes
- 3 New Carrots
- 3 Spring Onions
- 2 Garlic Cloves
- 1 bunch of Basil
- 1 tbsp of Balsamic Vinegar
- 2 tbsp of Extra Virgin Olive Oil
- 1 tsp of Chia Seeds
- Salt
- Black Pepper

Method

Step 1
Cut the carrots, courgettes and spring onion in Julienne in similar sizes.

Step 2
Boil the broad beans and peas separately in a little water, respectively, for 20 and 10 minutes from the boiling point. Let both legumes cool in their cooking water.

Step 3
Place carrots and spring onions in a pan with very little water to steam and cook with a lid for about 3 minutes; add the courgettes and continue cooking for around another 2-3 minutes. Once ready, drain gently and set aside.

Step 4
In a bowl, emulsify the oil with balsamic vinegar and a pinch of salt.

Step 5
Peel and dry the basil: break it up with your hands and set aside a few whole leaves for the decoration of the dishes.

Step 6
Drain the legumes and transfer them to a large salad bowl; add the boiled vegetables and sprinkle with the oil and vinegar emulsion; sprinkle with the chopped basil and the peeled and finely chopped garlic. Stir, distribute the salad on individual plates, sprinkle the chia seeds, black pepper, garnish with whole basil leaves and serve.

Nutrition Facts	Per Portion (358 g)
Energy	213 kcal
Protein	12g
Carbohydrate	28g
Sugars	12g
Fat	6g
Fatty Acids, Total Saturated	1g
Fibres	9g
Sodium	1054mg

Stuffed Zucchini with Lentils and a Herb Parmesan Crust

Stuffed Zucchine with Lentils and a Herb Parmesan Crust

Time: 50 minutes
4 Portions

Ingredients

- 1/2 cup Dry Brown or Green Lentils
- 2 tbsp Olive Oil
- 1/4 cup Red Onions, diced
- 4 Garlic Cloves, minced
- 2 cups Baby Spinach, roughly chopped
- 1 cup Tomato Sauce (homemade)
- 1/4 tbsp Chilli Flakes
- Salt and Pepper
- 100g Mozzarella Cheese, grated
- 50g Parmesan Cheese
- Italian Herbs (oregano, basil, thyme and rosemary, marjoram, parsley)
- 4 Zucchini cut lengthwise
- Cooking Spray

Method

Step 1

Rinse the lentils under running water for 1 minute thoroughly and allow them to soak in a small bowl for 10 minutes.

Bring 2 cups of water to a boil, add the lentils and allow them to cook for 10-15 minutes or until al-dente. Keep in mind. If your lentils are older, they may require several additional minutes. Drain the lentils in a strainer and rinse with cold water to stop them from cooking further.

Step 2

Position a rack in the centre of the oven and preheat the oven to 200°C. Spray a baking dish with cooking spray. Using a measure of 1 teaspoon, scoop out the centre of the zucchini, leaving a thick border on all sides. Line the zucchini in the prepared baking dish, skin side down; set aside.

Step 3

Heat the olive oil in a skillet over medium-high heat. Add the onions and allow to cook for 3-4 minutes or until they start to brown. Add the garlic and let cook for 30 seconds. Add in the baby spinach and the lentils and let the spinach just begin to wilt. Stir in the tomato sauce and let it heat all the way through, about 1-2 minutes. Add the chilli flakes, check for seasonings, season to taste.

Step 4

Divide the lentil mixture into the prepared zucchini. Top with mozzarella cheese, parmesan and herbs. Cover the baking dish with foil and bake for 30-35 minutes. You can remove the foil during the last 2 minutes of baking and turn on the broiler if you want the cheese to be bubbly.

Nutrition Facts	Per Portion (308 g)
Energy	262 kcal
Protein	18g
Carbohydrate	21g
Sugars	6g
Fat	13g
Fatty Acids, Total Saturated	6g
Fibres	3g
Sodium	1012mg

Cauliflower Pizza with Mushrooms

Time: 40 minutes
4 Portions

Ingredients

- 1 Cauliflower, large
- 3 Garlic Cloves, minced
- 2 tbsp Parmesan Cheese
- 1 Egg
- 100g Mozzarella Cheese
- 50g Tomato Sauce
- Salt
- 1/2 tbsp of Oregano
- 1/2 tbsp of Dehydrated Basil
- 120g of Mushrooms, finely sliced

Method

Step 1
Preheat the oven to 180ºC.
In a processor, mince the already cooked cauliflower (It is best if you cook for 4 minutes in the microwave without water). Then transfer the dough to a cloth to drain excess water. Now, transfer again to a bowl.

Step 2
Add the minced garlic, salt, oregano, parmesan cheese and the egg and mix well. Open the dough in a pizza tray. Bake for 20 minutes at 180°C.

Step 3
Once ready, remove from the oven and spread the tomato sauce, mozzarella, mushrooms and basil.
Add more oregano too. You can add tomatoes and onion if you like.

Return to the oven to melt the cheese for about 15 minutes

Remove and serve immediately.

Nutrition Facts	Per Portion (312g)
Energy	175 kcal
Protein	14g
Carbohydrate	10g
Sugars	4g
Fat	10g
Fatty Acids, Total Saturated	6g
Fibres	4g
Sodium	492mg

Spicy Red Lentil and Carrots Soup

Time: 40 minutes
3 Portions

Ingredients

- 1 tbsp Olive Oil
- 1 Onion (195g), large and finely chopped
- 1 Celery Stalk, finely chopped
- 4 Garlic Cloves, minced
- Coriander Leaves (handful), with removed stems and finely chopped
- 1 tsp (heaped) Curry Powder
- 1 tsp (heaped) Ground Cumin
- 1/4 tsp Red Chilli Flakes, dried
- 3 Carrots (415g), large and topped, tailed, and peeled, then roughly chopped
- 400g Canned Tomatoes, chopped
- 900ml Vegetable Stock
- 100g Red Split Lentils
- 1/4 tsp Sea Salt
- 1/4 tsp Ground Black Pepper
- 1 tbsp Greek Yoghurt and Coriander Leaves to serve (optional)

Method

Step 1
Heat the olive oil in a large saucepan. Add the chopped onion and celery and cook for about 10 minutes, stirring occasionally. Add the minced garlic. The chopped coriander stems along with ¼ teaspoon of dried red chilli flakes, curry powder and ground cumin. Stir well and cook for just one minute, any longer, and the spices will burn.

Step 2
Add the chopped carrots and pour in the chopped tomatoes and the vegetable stock.

Stir everything together, then add the lentils. Stir well, reduce the heat and simmer, covered, for about 30 minutes. The soup is ready once the carrots are tender and the lentils are cooked.

Step 3
Blend the soup with a hand-held blender until it is smooth. Finely chop the coriander leaves. Serve it with a good dollop of Greek yoghurt, chopped coriander and some low-carb bread.

Nutrition Facts	Per Portion (366 g)
Energy	243 kcal
Protein	13g
Carbohydrate	41g
Sugars	14g
Fat	5g
Fatty Acids, Total Saturated	1g
Fibres	6g
Sodium	1282mg

Courgettes, Peas, Cannellini Beans and Pesto Soup

Time: 25 minutes
4 Portions

Ingredients

- 1 tbsp of Olive Oil
- 2 Garlic Clove, sliced
- 500g Courgettes, quartered lengthwise and chopped
- 200g Frozen Peas
- 400g Canned Cannellini Beans, drained and rinsed
- 1 litre of Hot Vegetable Stock
- 2 tbsp of Basil Pesto
- 1 Onion, chopped

Method

STEP 1
Heat the oil in a large saucepan. Cook the garlic for a few seconds, then add the onion and courgettes and cook for 3 minutes until they start to soften. Stir in peas and cannellini beans, pour on the hot stock and cook for a further 3 minutes. Let the soup simmer (I normally let it simmer for about 15-20minutes) until it reaches your preferred consistency.

STEP 2
Stir the pesto through the soup with some seasoning, then ladle it into bowls and serve with crusty low-carb bread, if you like.

Nutrition Facts	Per Portion (1119 g)
Energy	413 kcal
Protein	30g
Carbohydrate	42g
Sugars	10g
Fat	15g
Fatty Acids, Total Saturated	5g
Fibres	8g
Sodium	400mg

Desserts

Keto Strawberry Cheesecake

Keto Strawberry Cheesecake

Time: 20 minutes (8 hours in total to set)
20 Portions

Ingredients

- 50g Almond Flour
- 50g Coconut Flour
- 25g Desiccated Coconut
- 85g Butter, melted
- 300g ricotta,softened to room temperature
- 200g Sour Cream, at room temperature
- 2 tbsp Erythritol
- 2 tsp Vanilla Extract
- 3 Eggs, large and at room temperature

Mixed Berries Coulis
- 100g Frozen Mixed Berries
- 3 tbsp Erythritol
- 50ml Water

Method

Step 1
Preheat the oven to 180°C.

Make the crust: Grease an 8" or 9" round baking tray, and cover the bottom and edges with foil. In a medium bowl, mix together the flours, coconut, and butter. Press the crust into the bottom and a little up the sides of the prepared pan. Place the tray in the fridge while you make the filling.

Step 2
Make the filling: In a large bowl, beat the ricotta and sour cream together, then beat in the erythritol and vanilla. Add the eggs one at a time, mixing after each addition. Spread the filling evenly over the crust.

Step 3
Place cheesecake in a deep roasting pan and set it on the middle rack of the oven. Carefully pour enough boiling water into the roasting pan to come halfway up the sides of the tray. Bake for 1 hour to 1 hour 20 minutes, until it only slightly jiggles in the centre. Turn off the oven, but leave the cake in the oven with the door slightly ajar to cool slowly for an hour.

Step 4
Remove the tray from the water bath and take off the foil, then let chill in the fridge for at least five hours or overnight. Slice and garnish with strawberries or with the Mixed Berries Coulis.

Step 5
To make the coulis, simply heat up the frozen berries with erythritol and water. Let it boil for about 5 minutes, reduce to simmer for another 5 minutes. Let it cool down before you add it to the cheesecake.

Nutrition Facts	Per Portion (62 g)
Energy	173 kcal
Protein	4g
Carbohydrate	5g
Sugars	2g
Fat	15g
Fatty Acids, Total Saturated	8g
Fibres	1g
Sodium	67mg

Aubergine and Coconut Brownie

Time: 30 minutes
4 Portions

Ingredients

- 1 tbsp of 90% Cocoa
- 2 Eggs
- 1 tsp Instant Coffee
- 1 tsp of Baking Powder
- 3 tbsp of Coconut Flour
- 2 tbsp of Erythritol or Xylitol
- 1 Aubergine, medium and sliced
- 20g Red Berries

Method

Step 1
Place the aubergine with the peel in the microwave until it gets darker for about 5-6 minutes.

Step 2
Then put all the ingredients in a blender and blend until it becomes homogeneous. Put the baking powder in the last.

Step 3
Grease the pan and bake at 180°C for 20 minutes.

Tip: If you want to make a sauce, it can be made with cocoa and coconut milk. This will make the brownie quite moist. Then just put shredded coconut and red berries on top and leave it in the fridge.

Nutrition Facts	Per Portion (52 g)
Energy	82 kcal
Protein	4g
Carbohydrate	7g
Sugars	1g
Fat	4g
Fatty Acids, Total Saturated	1g
Fibres	3g
Sodium	123mg

Banana & Chocolate Low Carb Cake

Time: 45 minutes
16 Portions

Ingredients

- 4 Bananas, large (I used three with the mixture) and one (chopped) to put on top
- 5 Eggs, small
- 80g of Desiccated Coconut
- 80g Almond Flour
- 1 tbsp Coconut Oil
- 1 tbsp Xylitol
- 1½1/2 tbsp Chocolate, powdered 70%
- 1 tbsp of Baking Powder

Method

Step 1
Preheat your oven to 180°C. Cut the bananas to place at the bottom of the cake.

Step 2
Beat everything in the blender until you get a homogeneous consistency. Add the baking powder last and only stir in.

* The bananas must be very ripe, so the sweet will stand out more in the cake!

Step 3
Assembling: spread a medium form of pudding with butter and almond flour, put some xylitol and the finely chopped banana slices. Pour the mixture over and bake for 20 minutes. Then just put the grated coconut on top.

Nutrition Facts	Per Portion (46 g)
Energy	101 kcal
Protein	2g
Carbohydrate	8g
Sugars	4g
Fat	7g
Fatty Acids, Total Saturated	3g
Fibres	2g
Sodium	49mg

Carrots & Coconut Low Carb Cake

Time: 40 minutes
20 Portions

Ingredients

- 4 Eggs
- 3 Carrots (270g)
- 3/4 large cups Coconut Oil
- 150g of Almond Flour
- 150g of Coconut Flour
- 1 tbsp Baking Powder
- 20g Erythritol

Method

Step 1
Preheat the oven to 210°C.

Grate the carrots.

Step 2
Put all the liquid ingredients + erythritol in the blender and then add the carrot little by little. Add the almond flour and then the coconut flour until the dough is homogeneous. When finished, add the baking powder and stir with a spoon.

Step 3
Place to bake in a greased baking tray for about 30 minutes. Test with the toothpick before removing. Then just put the dehydrated coconut on top.

Nutrition Facts	Per Portion (34 g)
Energy	148 kcal
Protein	3g
Carbohydrate	5g
Sugars	1g
Fat	13g
Fatty Acids, Total Saturated	7g
Fibres	3g
Sodium	36mg

Frozen Mixed Berries and Yogurt Tart

Time: : 5 minutes prep and 30 minutes in the freezer
5 Portions

Ingredients

- 600g of Greek Yoghurt
- 300g Frozen Mixed Berries
- 30g Desiccated Coconut
- 1 tbsp of Xylitol
- 1 tsp Vanilla Extract

Method

In a blender or food processor add all the ingredients until it is well mixed together. Freeze for about 30 minutes. Add any desired fruits and some coconuts on top. It is ready to serve!

Nutrition Facts	Per Portion (189 g)
Energy	223 kcal
Protein	7g
Carbohydrate	14g
Sugars	9g
Fat	16g
Fatty Acids, Total Saturated	11g
Fibres	1g
Sodium	82mg

Passion Fruit Mousse with Yogurt

Time: 20 minutes preparation (4 hours in the fridge)
8 Portions

Ingredients

- 4 Passion Fruits
- 500ml Greek Yoghurt
- 4 tbsp Erythritol
- 200ml Cream
- 75ml Passion Fruit Juice, concentrated
- 1 pack (35g) of Gelatin, organic and unflavoured
- 50ml Water to dissolve gelatin

Coulis

- 2 Passion Fruits
- 2 tbsp Erythritol
- 50ml Passion Fruit Juice, concentrated

Tip: If you cannot find Passion Fruit, you can use Mixed Berries instead

Method

Step 1
Dissolve the gelatin in 50ml of cold water and leave it for about 5 minutes - the gelatin will absorb the water. Always add gelatine to liquid, not the other way around. Stir briskly until thoroughly mixed. Bring it to microwave for 10 seconds or bring to low heat until it is fully dissolved.

Step 2
Whip the cream with three tablespoons of erythritol until it is firm.

Step 3
Slice four passion fruits in half and use a spoon to scoop out the delicious pulp of the passion fruit. Mix passion fruit pulp, concentrate juice, gelatin and Greek yoghurt until smooth.

Step 4
Combine whipped cream, passion fruit and Greek yoghurt until smooth again. Place in the fridge to set for 4 hours.

Step 5
Cut two passion fruits in half and scrape the pips and juice into a bowl. Cook it with two tablespoon erythritol until it is fully melted and reduced.

Top each mousse with a spoonful of passion fruit and serve.

Nutrition Facts	Per Portion (198 g)
Energy	170 kcal
Protein	9 g
Carboydrate	24 g
Sugars	7 g
Fat	11 g
Fatty Acids, Total Saturated	7 g
Fibers	1 g
Sódium	64 mg

Mixed Berries Healthy Trifle

Mixed Berries Healthy Trifle

Time: 45 minutes
15 Portions

Ingredients

- 45ml Orange or other fruit flavoured liquor (like Cointreau), or apple, orange or other fruit juice (or 2 tbsp brandy)
- 11g Gelatine Powder, organic
- 750ml Cranberry Juice, original
- 2 small baskets of Strawberries,halved
- 1 small basket of Blueberries
- 1 small basket of Raspberries

CAKE LAYER

- 115g Almond Flour
- 20g Coconut Flour
- 30g Erythritol (or regular granulated)
- 5g Baking Powder
- 3 Eggs, large
- 35g Coconut oil (measured solid, then melted)
- 1 tsp Vanilla Extract

Method

Step 1: Cake
Preheat the oven to 180 degrees C. Line the bottom of a 23 cm round or 20 cm square tray with parchment paper.
In a large bowl, mix together the almond flour, coconut flour, erythritol, and baking powder.
Stir in the eggs. Whisk together the melted coconut oil and vanilla extract, then stir that in as well. Mix well until a dough forms.
Transfer the dough to the lined tray and press in evenly. Bake for 25-30 minutes until the top is golden and firm. Let the cake cool to room temperature, then cut into 2.5 cm cubes.

Step 2: Cranberry Jelly
Put half (325ml) of the cranberry juice into a saucepan over medium heat. Bring to a simmer, then turn off the stove.
Meanwhile, put remaining room temperature cranberry juice into a bowl. Sprinkle gelatine all across the surface (don't dump in one place). Whisk until mostly dissolved.
Pour in hot cranberry juice. Whisk until the gelatin is fully dissolved. Proceed with the recipe – jelly will be warm.

Step 3: Jelly Layer 1
Pour half (325ml) the cranberry jelly liquid carefully over the cake in the trifle dishes.
Refrigerate uncovered for 1.5 hours until it is partly set – still quite soft, but not watery (i.e. if you gently place a strawberry on it, it will stay on the surface).

Pour remaining jelly in a bowl and leave it on the counter (do not refrigerate). Meanwhile, make the custard.

Step 4: Homemade Custard
Bring the plant-based milk, 25g, erythritol and vanilla to a simmer in a large saucepan over medium heat. Do not boil.
In a large bowl, whisk together the remaining 25g erythritol and yolks, then whisk in the cornflour until smooth.

Ingredients

CREAM

- 315ml Cream, heavy/ thickened
- 25g Erythritol
- 1 tsp Vanilla Extract

HOMEMADE THICK CUSTARD

- 350ml Plant-Based Milk
- 50g Erythritol
- 1 tsp Vanilla Bean Paste (or extract)
- 2 Egg Yolks
- 40g Cornflour/Cornstarch, (gluten-free)

Method

Once incorporated and smooth, pour back into the saucepan. Return saucepan to the stove over low heat. Whisk constantly until it becomes thick and custardy – this will happen quite quickly, about 45 seconds (i.e. it is liquid when you start, then suddenly it thickens).

Once thickened, remove immediately from heat – it will continue to thicken.

Pour into a bowl and cover with cling wrap, pressing onto the surface. Leave on the counter until the trifle is ready to layer with custard.

Step 5: Custard Later

Remove trifle from the fridge. Spoon over the custard, smooth surface, press on the glass to seal (stops jelly bleed). Refrigerate for 1 hour until the surface has firmed up a bit – just enough to hold the jelly (jelly is soft, so the custard doesn't need to be fully set).

Put remaining jelly in the fridge at the same time (to thicken a bit, but not too much, so you get a neat, clear layer of jelly).

CHECK jelly at 30 minutes, just to ensure it's not setting too fast.

Step 6: Jelly Layer 2

Remove trifle and jelly from the fridge. Jelly should be sloppy.

Carefully spoon over the jelly, smooth surface. Scatter over 1 small basket halved strawberries (or half each raspberry and strawberry).

Refrigerate for 3 hours+ (can leave in the fridge for 48 hours, until ready to assemble).

Step 7: Assembling

Cream: Beat cream, erythritol and vanilla until softly whipped.

Once the jelly is set, just before serving, top with cream, then pile over the remaining berries.

Dust with icing sugar.

Nutrition Facts	Per Portion (147 g)
Energy	297 kcal
Protein	6g
Carbohydrate	18g
Sugars	8g
Fat	24g
Fatty Acids, Total Saturated	9g
Fibres	3g
Sodium	211mg

Snacks

Blueberries Muffin

Time: 25 minutes
8 Portions

Ingredients

- 100g of Fine Almond Flour
- 50g Coconut Flour
- 90ml Almond Milk
- 25g Xylitol
- 2 Eggs
- 50g of Blueberries (if you don't have it, use other types of berries – blackberries, raspberries, etc.)
- 1/2 tbsp of Baking Powder
- 1 tbsp Vanilla Extract
- 1 pinch of Salt

Method

Step 1
Preheat your oven to 180°C.

In a bowl add the eggs, almond milk, vanilla extract and xylitol. Mix well to incorporate the ingredients.

Step 2
Add almond flour, coconut flour and baking powder. Stir until you have a homogeneous mass.

Step 3
Add the blueberries and mix.

Transfer the dough to the muffin tray.

Step 4
Bake for approximately 15 minutes. The time may vary according to the oven. So keep an eye out and take the toothpick test to see if it's ready!

Let it cool and enjoy!

Nutrition Facts	Per Portion (53 g)
Energy	138 kcal
Protein	5g
Carbohydrate	7g
Sugars	1g
Fat	9g
Fatty Acids, Total Saturated	0g
Fibres	4g
Sodium	329mg

Papaya and Yogurt Mousse

Time: 5 minutes
2 Portions

Ingredients

- 200g Greek Yoghurt
- Papaya without pips
- 1 tbsp of Crème de Cassis (if it is a special occasion!)

Method

There are two ways to do this:

1. Add the yoghurt and papaya to a blender and blend it until it reaches a smooth consistency. Serve at room temperature.

2. Put the yoghurt in the freezer the day before you will use it. The next day blend it with the papaya. This will be very refreshing and a great summer option.

If it is a special occasion, you can use this as a nice dessert option, just add a tablespoon of Crème de Cassis and enjoy!

Nutrition Facts	Per Portion (189 g)
Energy	205 kcal
Protein	6g
Carbohydrate	14g
Sugars	11g
Fat	14g
Fatty Acids, Total Saturated	10g
Fibres	1g
Sodium	74mg

Beetroot Hummus

Time: : Less than 10 min
4 Portions

Ingredients

- 300g Chickpeas
- 2 Lemons
- Salt and Pepper
- 1 tsp of Sumac
- 1 tsp of Tahini
- 2 Garlic Cloves
- 1 tsp of Cumin Powder
- 2 Beetroots, small and cooked
- Raw Vegetables, such as Carrots, Cucumber, Celery, Cherry Tomatoes, etc.

Method

Step 1
Cook the chickpeas just with water and salt for 40 minutes.

Step 2
Put the chickpeas with the juice of the two lemons, beetroots, garlic, Sumac, Tahini and Cumin powder in a blender. Blend it until homogeneous.

Step 3
Season with salt and pepper to your taste and keep it in the fridge.

Nutrition Facts	Per Portion (123 g)
Energy	109 kcal
Protein	5g
Carbohydrate	13g
Sugars	2g
Fat	4g
Fatty Acids, Total Saturated	1g
Fibres	4g
Sodium	1211mg

Antioxidant Popcorn

Time: 10 minutes
3 Portions

Ingredients

- 1 tbsp of Olive Oil
- 25g Popcorn Kernels
- 100g Dark Chocolate 70%

Method

Step 1
Pop the popcorn kernels in a saucepan with a tightfitting lid for 4 minutes.

Step 2
Melt the dark chocolate in a bain-marie.

STEP 3
Pour the dark chocolate onto the popcorn. Now just enjoy!

Nutrition Facts	Per Portion (45 g)
Energy	264 kcal
Protein	4g
Carbohydrate	22g
Sugars	8g
Fat	18g
Fatty Acids, Total Saturated	9g
Fibres	5g
Sodium	7mg

Keto Smoothie

Time: 5 minutes
1 Portion

Ingredients

- 80g Cold Avocado
- 2 tbsp Cocoa Powder 85%
- 200ml Almond Milk
- 1 tbsp of Xylitol
- 1 tsp of Flaxseeds
- 1 tsp of Sunflower Seeds

Method

Just add all the ingredients to a blender and blend until it reaches a smoothie consistency. Serve immediately.

Nutrition Facts	Per Portion (325 g)
Energy	347 kcal
Protein	7g
Carbohydrate	35g
Sugars	1g
Fat	25g
Fatty Acids, Total Saturated	2g
Fibres	8g
Sodium	153mg

Antioxidant Juice

Time: 5 minutes
1 Portion

Ingredients

- 30g Kale
- 30g Mango
- Kiwi
- 30g Spinach
- 1 tsp of Flaxseeds or Chia
- Ginger to your taste
- 200ml Water

Method

Just add all the ingredients to a blender and blend for a few minutes. Serve immediately.

Tip:
The juice will be great if you freeze the ingredients.

Nutrition Facts	Per Portion (350g)
Energy	133 kcal
Protein	5g
Carbohydrate	18g
Sugars	8g
Fat	6g
Fatty Acids, Total Saturated	1g
Fibres	8g
Sodium	29mg

Healthy food, real food, is in the
center of Priscilla and Raquel's life. With this in mind,
can you imagine the importance of a cookbook
nutritious for a lover of gastronomy and
healthy food and for a nutritionist.

Full Kitchen has over 50 recipes that will
inspire you to start cooking. And as a bonus you
will eat well calculated and balanced dishes for a
super experienced nutritionist for life.

Priscilla has traveled a lot around the world. she will
bring a little piece from many corners of it in this book.
her passion for cuisine is remarkably unique.
The recipes in this book are adaptations of many
recipes. from her personal page where she shares
others healthy recipes and tips.

Raquel made the choices of recipes that would be
more suitable for a fantastic and different eating plan.
The idea is for everyone to enjoy Priscilla's creations
following a balanced diet, having results
incredible and a beautiful and healthy body.